MW00425719

nickel and dime your way to wealth

WEALTHBUILDING ON ANY INCOME

Deborah Owens

Owens Media Group
Columbia, Maryland

Owens Media Group LLC
9250 Bendix Rd. N. Suite 745
Columbia, Md 21045
www.deborahowens.com

Ordering Information:

Quantity sales. Special discounts are available on quantity purchases by corporations, associations, and others. For details, contact the "Special Sales Department" at the address above.

Contents

Dedication

This book is dedicated to the Super Savers:

Osceola McCarty and Mr. Earl.

Your generosity and spirit of optimism

are evidence of faith in action.

Your stories changed my life and the lives of countless

others.

Thank you for paying it forward.

Introduction

HE CALLED IN regularly to the weekly public radio program that I host in Baltimore, and he changed my life. His name is Mr. Earl.

After two decades in the financial services industry as a financial consultant and vice president at Fidelity Investments, I had wanted a change. The investment industry focused on "high net worth" clients; I wanted to make investing accessible to people of all income levels. So in 1996, I created the radio show "Real Money" with the purpose of helping "real people" take control of their finances. Every week since then, the program has devoted a full hour to an investment topic, featuring authors and financial experts, and taking questions from listeners on the air.

All the experts I interview tend to convey a recurring theme: Invest for the long term and don't worry about short-term fads or market volatility. Yet, in spite of this advice, listeners continued to call with excuses for why the experts' advice wouldn't work for them. After several years of hosting the program, I could no longer hide my frustration. The excuse that sent me over the edge was, "Investing is for the rich." My reply? "Investing is how you get rich." I could sense I was morphing into a talk show caricature. While the first five years were exciting and I looked forward to each broadcast, I was becoming the host who thought every question was dumb and wanted to hang up on callers. I prayed for patience to continue giving my listeners the encouragement and practical advice our show had been recognized for. Instinctively, I knew they would learn by example from others like them. Forget the experts. I needed to hear from real people, the kind of folks everyone could relate to. That's how the "Real Money, Real People" segments began.

These segments grew out of open phone nights when listeners

called in with their questions or concerns about investing. I encouraged them to respond to other callers if they'd had a similar experience and could share how they dealt with it. It was amazing to listen to "real people" share their experiences about finding financial advisors, or making their first investment and watching how it performed over time.

For several years, Mr. Earl called often, and with great suggestions. Typically, he made provocative investment recommendations such as "Miss Debbie, I think the listeners should invest in defense stocks." Each time he called, the studio telephone lines lit up. Because of that, I asked him to be my guest on the first "Real Money, Real People" segment. He was flattered and extremely humble about his financial accomplishments. The only thing I knew about him was that he worked for a bank.

I began the interview with the question, "Mr. Earl, what was your first investment?"

He replied, "One of the first stocks I invested in was IBM. I scraped up the money to buy two shares."

"Do you still own IBM stock?"

"Yes," he said. "Those two shares have become 250 shares through the dividend reinvestment program."

"Wow. Who recommended that particular stock?" I asked.

"I purchased IBM in 1981 because I saw it mentioned on television and I knew it was a big company. The broker was upset that I was buying such a small amount, but he reduced his commission to 10 dollars—that was a big deal at the time."

When the phones kept ringing with questions for Mr. Earl, I knew the "Real Money, Real People" segment would be the answer to my prayers.

This interview with Mr. Earl also began a relationship that has inspired me to continue helping others become financially empowered. You see, Mr. Earl helped me gain the insight I needed to finally make a shift in my own thinking about personal finance.

In the first edition of this book, I shared how my outlook about finances changed. Several years after writing the book, I finally recognized what Mr. Earl had come to recognize at the bank, despite having no special financial training—wealthy people think, act, and manage their finances differently than most people. Mr. Earl was able to observe that financially successful people had different attitudes, beliefs, and behaviors that allowed them to achieve financial independence.

In my most recent book, A Purse of Your Own, published by Simon and Schuster, I researched and identified seven attitudes and behaviors, which I called "the seven wealthy habits." I have incorporated them into this latest edition of Nickel and Dime Your Way to Wealth to further illustrate how these same principles allowed Mr. Earl to achieve such financial success. In sharing Mr. Earl's remarkable story, this book provides a roadmap for building wealth on any income. His story has put a face on financial empowerment and has inspired thousands of people I've taught at workshops and conferences to take control of their financial future.

If Mr. Earl can do it, you can too!

-chapter 1-
Nickel and Diming

What I know now is Mr. Earl observed the same wealthy habits that I discuss in my book A Purse of Your Own and then applied them to achieve personal wealth. Those seven habits are fundamental to changing your behavior and making your money work for you, and I discuss them throughout this book. But at first, having him as a guest on my radio show, I wasn't quite sure exactly what he knew about growing his wealth. So I decided to find out.

Knowledge Correctly Applied Is Power

Intrigued by Mr. Earl, I naturally wanted to know more about him and the types of investments he'd made over the years. So I offered to conduct a portfolio review, a process I used in my previous career as a financial advisor. Mr. Earl accepted my offer and invited me to his home.

Mr. Earl lives in a tree-lined neighborhood in one of Baltimore's famous row houses. The homes, designed by a renowned architect, have flagstone exteriors complemented by manicured landscaping.

He greeted me at the door and introduced me to Beverly, his wife of 36 years. Mr. Earl took great pride in showing me his home improvement projects in their modestly furnished home. In particular, he had paneled part of the living room and lamented that it still needed a few finishing touches.

The Portfolio Review

Settling down at the dining room table, I took out a legal pad and calculator, and prepared to review Mr. Earl's portfolio, which discloses how someone's financial journey began and has progressed. The process reveals a lot about a person's investment experience—and I wanted to learn about his. He took out an accordion file and handed me statements from each of his main accounts. I wrote these headings on my legal pad: Date of Purchase, Security Description, Type of Account, and Market Value.

Mr. Earl's Non-retirement Accounts

We began by listing these four elements under the heading Non-retirement. Mr. Earl handed me the confirmation statement from his first purchase of IBM stock, which he had mentioned during his radio interview. He also showed me the dividend reinvestment statement from IBM. Then we listed 963 shares of "Employer Bank," the stock from his employer that he purchased through payroll deduction. In 2001, the time of my visit, it had a current value of approximately $30,000. He also held several individual stocks in odd amounts: 113 shares of Duke Energy, 122 shares of Exxon, 5.33 shares of Bell South, and 54.38 shares of Colgate Palmolive. The reason for these odd amounts became clear to me later.

In addition to individual stocks, Mr. Earl had a number of mutual fund holdings. His first mutual fund investment was in the Fidelity Destiny II Fund, purchased through a broker. Through this contractual arrangement, he committed to invest $25 a month for 15 years. Although it carried a sales charge of 8.5 percent, it was now valued at more than $38,000.

He also purchased the no-load Fidelity Fund after dumping the Fidelity Magellan fund because of its recent lackluster performance. But he wasn't happy with his decision to sell the Magellan Fund. You see, portfolio manager Peter Lynch was one of his investment idols and although Mr. Lynch no longer managed the fund, Mr. Earl felt remorseful because it had been an exceptional performer in his portfolio. I also learned that I might have played a role in his decision to sell the fund. He had called into the radio show to ask my opinion and I suggested that it might have run its course. I was surprised to learn that he respected my analysis of the situation, and I realized that our radio show was providing listeners with information they used in making investment decisions.

I noted that his investments were well diversified between stocks, mutual funds, and money market accounts. In fact, his portfolio mirrored those of many wealthy clients I had assisted throughout my career.

Mr. Earl's Retirement Accounts

Then we shifted to his Retirement portfolios. He'd invested a sizeable amount in his employer-sponsored 401(k) retirement plan, which held more shares of Employer Bank stock. He'd invested his annual IRA contributions in the Legg Mason Value and Special Investment Trust funds managed by Bill Miller, another outstanding portfolio manager. I later learned that Legg Mason had offices in Mr. Earl's employer's building, which helped explain why he initially invested his IRA contributions in its mutual funds. Convenience aside, Mr. Earl believed in "betting on the jockey," meaning investing in accounts with a portfolio manager who had a winning track record.

After reviewing his portfolio, I noticed that his IRAs were valued at more than his 401(k). This rarely happens, because most people can contribute up to 15 percent of their salaries to their 401(k)s, and in some cases their employer matches a percentage. In comparison, at the time of Mr. Earl's portfolio review, the maximum contribution to IRAs was a few thousand dollars a year.

Mr. Earl's Investments for His Children

Next, we looked at the investments he'd made on behalf of his three children, who were all over 30 years old. Each child had shares of Exxon, Colgate Palmolive, Bell Atlantic (Verizon), and Lucent Technology (Alcatel-Lucent). The number of shares in each stock varied from 7 to 75.

He had enrolled all of the accounts in Stock Dividend Reinvestment Programs, also known as DRIP plans. I asked Mr. Earl if his children knew about these investments and he said, "Yes. But I manage their accounts and hope that one day they will follow my example."

How It Added Up

After listing and calculating the value of the holdings in Mr. Earl's portfolio, I determined how his investments were allocated between stocks, bonds, and cash. This allowed me to research his portfolio's industry weightings and make sure he wasn't heavily exposed in a specific sector or company within his portfolio. Then I reviewed how his investments performed relative to similar investments over the same holding periods. Finally, I needed to determine if his portfolio met his objectives for future planning.

I realized Mr. Earl had no idea how much his overall portfolio was worth. After he pulled investment statements from every nook and cranny in his house, I used them to calculate the total value of his investment portfolio—$434,000 in 2001. Not bad for a bank employee. But I still needed to know how much Mr. Earl earned at the bank and when he would retire to determine whether his portfolio would meet his objectives.

Nickel and Dimin' in Practice

I plunged in, asking, "Mr. Earl, how long before you can retire?"

"Oh, I plan on retiring in two years when I turn 65. That's when I'll collect Social Security," he said.

"What's your position at the bank and how much do you earn?" I asked.

"I'm the parking attendant and have been for 33 years. I earn just about $2,000 a month," he replied. "You see, I don't have much of an education. I was labeled a slow learner and dropped out of school in the eighth grade. That didn't stop me, though. I went to Frederick Douglas High School at night and finally earned my high school diploma. When I started working at the bank as a custodian, I earned $70 a week. I got a promotion to the parking attendant job and really enjoy it. I'm responsible for making sure the bank patrons can find a parking space when they visit the bank. I've had a great run."

I almost fell out of my chair. "How in the world were you able to save this much money as a parking attendant?" I asked.

"Nickel and dimin'," said Mr. Earl.

"Nickel and dimin'," I repeated. "What is nickel and dimin'?"

Mr. Earl explained, "There are two parts to 'nickel and dimin'. There are nickel-and-dime jobs that pay $10 or $20 every week. That's what I earned from cleaning the Italian bakery shop and jewelry store, and landscaping outside the bridal shop across from the bank. The second part is nickel-and-dime investments. The $20 or $30 extra I earned each week added up to over $100 a month."

And that's how he scraped up the first few hundred dollars to buy the IBM stock—investing the money from his nickel-and-dime jobs in blue chip stocks.

Now it all made sense. His shares of Baltimore Gas & Electric, IBM, and Colgate Palmolive had initially been purchased by nickel and dimin'. The odd numbers of shares of stock that he owned resulted from buying one or two shares at a time and reinvesting the dividends.

Wealthy vs. Working Class

In Mr. Earl's early years on that parking lot, a bank executive took him aside and told him that he couldn't go far with a limited education, and suggested he should save a few dollars toward his future. That was the first of many pieces of advice he received from his interactions with bank customers and employees. Mr. Earl took that advice to heart and acted on it.

"When I watched the customers go to their safe-deposit boxes and take out their stock certificates, I made a goal that I would own 1,000 shares of stock," Mr. Earl had told me. Every day, he greeted the patrons of the bank with a warm smile and a kind word. Sometimes they put important papers in their safe-deposit boxes; other times they spent an hour or two talking with their private bankers. Mr. Earl observed that when wealthy people needed to borrow money, they used their stock certificates as collateral for a loan. That helped him understand the financial security that owning stocks represented. He wanted the choices that stock ownership provided. Mr. Earl observed that wealthy people think differently!

Mr. Earl also noticed other differences between the wealthy and the working class. For example, wealthy people visit the bank at odd times of the month to deposit several checks, or interest payments from their bonds, or dividend checks from their stocks. Working class people deposit their paychecks either weekly or biweekly like clockwork. Retired working class people only visit the bank the first of the month to cash their Social Security checks. Wealthy retired customers visit the bank to deposit dividend checks from their stocks and redeem interest coupons from their bonds. Their money works for them so they don't have to work.

Author Keith Cameron Smith explains it this way:

Very poor people think day to day.

Poor people think week to week.

Middle class people think month to month.

Rich people think year to year.

Very rich people think decade to decade.

The fact is that wealthy people think generation to generation

What Mr. Earl Taught Me

Mr. Earl's accomplishments held extreme significance for me. Finally, someone could demonstrate that one's station in life did not determine what could be achieved.

You see, I had always believed that people simply needed access and a mechanism for investing. It goes against the common belief in Middle America that investing is for the rich, not how to get rich. Early in my career, I remember inviting average folks into marbled, plush-carpeted offices, and I saw how many felt intimidated by the environment. They associated it with being reserved for "rich people only." And while conducting a seminar at a university, a college graduate told me that investing was like gambling or "magic." Mr. Earl validated what I had always believed: Investing is not just for the rich; it's how you get rich!

How could I share that story through Mr. Earl's example? I didn't

want to divulge too much for fear that I could jeopardize his ano-
nymity. Of course, I should have known better than that. Mr. Earl
was proud of what he had accomplished, yet he didn't brag or boast.
Humility is his strong suit and he carried himself in that manner. In
fact, many of his coworkers said he was a little too humble. Watching him greet and attend to customers in the parking stall reminded
them of the days it was the only job available to a black man. But
Mr. Earl didn't allow himself to dwell on how he might be perceived
by other people. He had work to do and little time for stewing. So
he encouraged me to tell his story in detail so others could learn
how to "nickel and dime," too.

The Seven Wealthy Habits

What I know now is that Mr. Earl observed the same wealthy habits that I discuss in my book A Purse of Your Own and then applied
them to achieve personal wealth. Those seven habits are fundamental to changing your behavior and making your money work for you.
The seven habits are:

1. **Wealthy Outlook** – This is the habit of adding value to others
   and exceeding expectations. Wealthy people recognize that
   other people play an important part in creating their future
   each day. Having a wealthy outlook requires you to have an
   understanding of where you stand financially, including what
   you own and what you owe.

2. **Wealthy Vision** – Identify your skills, strengths, and talents
   so you will be able to leverage them to create value for others.

Your values also matter in order for you to build wealth, and it is important to understand what they are in order to stay your course.

3. **Wealthy Appetite** – Develop a thirst for knowledge and increase your financial acumen. Read as much as you can and find a mentor. This will allow you to build confidence, boost your knowledge, and be current on the economy and the financial markets

4. **Wealthy Focus** – Know your goals and the timelines needed to complete them. Be clear on what you need to do in order to stay on track financially.

5. **Wealthy Mindset** – The greatest risk is taking no risk at all. Learn how to turn problems into opportunities in order to take calculated risks. Wealthy people become wealthy by resisting the temptation to follow the crowd.

6. **Wealthy System** – Set up simple wealth-building systems that allow you to keep your finances in shape and to leverage the power of compounding.

7. **Wealthy Legacy** – Pay it forward to others. Help your family and friends become financially responsible and look for ways to help others incorporate the seven wealthy habits.

Nickel and Dimin'

Your station in life does not determine what you can achieve. Investing is not for the rich; it's how you get rich.

-chapter 2-

Give to Get

Wealthy Outlook—The Habit of Adding Value

It was a year later, and I had just arrived at the Department of Labor Headquarters in Washington, D.C. for an award ceremony honoring Mr. Earl. Although the building resembled a cement fortress on the outside, inside it was opulent with its marble foyer and hardwood-paneled rooms.

I was escorted to Mr. Earl's table where he was seated in a wheelchair, struggling to gain his composure. "Don't I look like a pitiful sight?" Mr. Earl asked, stricken by a case of gout the previous evening and unable to walk. His wife, his daughter, and one of his two sons also sat at the table. As I scanned the crowd—several hundred at least—I took note of the CEOs, scholars, and bureaucrats in attendance. They were all anticipating words of wisdom from the recipient of the first Osceola McCarty Super Saver Award.

Osceola McCarty, a washwoman from Mississippi, had accumulated $280,000 and donated $150,000 of it to the University of Mississippi. The Department of Labor wanted to encourage Americans to save for their future, so it designed a Super Saver Award to be presented to someone who exemplified the same attributes of Ms. McCarty. A selection committee had combed the nation to identify someone worthy of accepting this award. Mr. Earl fit the requirement perfectly.

As we assembled on stage and the assistant secretary of the Department of Labor prepared to give Mr. Earl the award, I filled with emotion when I stepped forward to introduce Mr. Earl. With extreme pleasure, I told the story of how this man from humble beginnings faced insurmountable circumstances and succeeded in spite of them. Mr. Earl then shared experiences that had shaped his life and told how he achieved his financial goals. By the time he finished his story, many eyes had watered, and the room roared with applause.

We presented Mr. Earl with a crystal statue and he beamed with pride. He felt uncomfortable accepting this award while in a wheelchair because it was totally out of character for him—a man who proudly had held more than 10 nickel-and-dime jobs at one time. This was the first time his gout had flared up to such a crippling degree, probably from all the excitement.

When I had spoken to Mr. Earl the day before, he never let on that he was in pain and could barely walk. He simply anticipated the exciting day lying ahead. Mr. Earl knew how to make the best of any situation; nothing could ruin this day for him. At 63 years old, he exhibited behavior that I believe is the secret to his success in life: He expected a positive outcome.

Mr. Earl's Money Story

"Labeled a slow learner as a young child, I was left behind as my classmates went to high school," Mr. Earl began his story that day. "At 13 years old, I found my first part-time job bagging groceries in Baltimore's Lexington Market stalls. I made enough money to help my mother with the household expenses and pay some of the tuition for my siblings who attended Catholic school," he continued. Being labeled a slow learner didn't prevent Mr. Earl from completing high school. He worked during the day and attended Frederick Douglas high school at night. Certainly his positive outlook helped him earn a high school diploma.

"My wise mother insisted that I save and tithe a portion of my pay. These early influences in stewardship and faith helped me establish my work ethic and habit of savings at a young age. I remember my mother telling me, 'Save something from your pay every week.' I knew my future job opportunities weren't promising and the few dollars I earned at the open-air market wouldn't be enough to support a family. So I worked several odd jobs from cutting lawns to cleaning the homes of the Catholic teachers at the school I'd attended. As a single man, I made it work.

"All that changed when I met a girl named Beverly at a church function. Eventually we got married and I needed something steady to support my family. My mother helped me find a janitorial job at a bank that her employer had told her about."

Most people would have considered this "port-a-job" position (as the janitorial position was called) menial. Mr. Earl viewed it as another open door. Eventually he was promoted to parking attendant, which presented him with the opportunity to interact with the bank's wealthy customers, as well as the stockbrokers and executives who had offices in the building. He performed this role with pride and a sense of authority. Mr. Earl's outlook allowed him to see a bright future from that parking lot.

To this day, Mr. Earl's warm smile and helpful disposition leave a positive impression with everyone he meets. This extraordinary parking lot attendant presents himself with an air of dignity and humility. His dry-cleaned windbreaker, starched shirts, and pressed khakis show the pride he takes in his appearance. And woe to people who park their cars in the bank lot with ulterior motives. As they're asked to leave, they receive a lecture from the "Mayor of Pennsylvania Avenue" who admonishes them for disrespecting the bank's posted parking policies.

Attitude for Success

As I sat next to Mr. Earl at the award ceremony, I realized that his receiving the Osceola McCarty Super Saver Award was destiny. You see, this book is not about how to get rich quick or how to make your fortune in the stock market. It's about the attitudes and behaviors needed to become successful in life. The first attitude is "outlook determines outcome."

Mr. Earl answered my prayers at a time when my frustration with my audiences' outlook was at an all-time high. My approach to "Real Money" had never been to provide the typical advice heard on television networks or read in newspapers. Instead, I likened myself to a skeptical cheerleader. I'd help demystify the technical jargon espoused by financial experts and provide listeners with the context to apply information to their own lives. Because of Mr. Earl, I realized that building wealth is an inside job. That meant that in order to have listeners act on the information being presented on the show, I had to make a connection with their hearts as well as their heads. They needed to "see and feel" someone in circumstances similar to theirs for the message to be real. Simply stated, their outlooks needed to be changed.

Do you believe the future is bright? Or are you focused on the bad economic news that you constantly see and hear in the news media? There will always be negative events to focus on—but only if you choose to.

Outlook Determines Outcome

If you change the way you look at things,
the things you look at change.
Wayne Dyer- Author

Change your outlook,
Change your outcome,
Change your income.

-chapter 3-
Your Gifts Will Pave The Way

Wealthy Vision: The Habit of Leveraging Your Unique Strengths

"I couldn't take the money from my children's mouths," Mr. Earl had explained. Years ago, Mr. Earl knew that to make his first investment, he had to find an additional source of income. His parking attendant's salary didn't leave much left over after he paid his bills, so he took stock of what he did have: location. He looked down Pennsylvania Avenue and saw part-time opportunities in gardening and cleaning to supplement his salary. If he looked carefully, he saw that almost every business on Pennsylvania Avenue had a need he could fill. His story illustrates how easy it is to look everywhere for answers when the solution is staring at us.

Why Don't People Invest?

In a recent survey of middle-income households, more than 40 percent of Americans admitted they had saved nothing toward retirement. Why? Because lack of exposure and access to an investment professional or company can be major impediments to building wealth. Non-investors often feel shame and apprehension because they haven't been exposed to the investment markets and therefore don't feel comfortable asking others for help.

Another reason people don't invest is because discussions around money and investing are considered taboo in many cultures. Certainly this lack of understanding and access prevented Ms. McCarty from broadening her investment portfolio sooner than she did. I think it's also one of the causes for the limited participation in many employer-sponsored retirement plans. Remember, Mr. Earl worked close to brokers and bankers, gaining access to investment information, yet he still waited many years to invest because of his ambivalence and his long-time belief that investing is for the rich.

Common Excuses

Every week, people call my radio show with reasons why they can't invest. "It's too complicated; how do I know where to invest?" and "I don't have enough money" are their most frequently voiced concerns. Let's look at these excues.

"It's Too Complicated"

If something seems too complicated, what's the remedy? Just begin to learn. Mr. Earl listened to the stockbrokers and the bank's customers while in the parking lot. They discussed different investments and he chatted them up to see what he could learn. He had access to a broker and got a sense of who might best fit his needs or give him a break because he was starting out with a little bit of money. Callers to my radio show often ask for a referral to a financial advisor or investment company. I suggest they use a similar approach to Mr. Earl's. No, I don't mean spending time in a parking lot, but rather chatting with financial advisors.

For example, in most communities, investment companies and financial advisors give free educational seminars. All they require is that attendees critique the event and provide their names, addresses, and telephone numbers. Seminars like these are held in neutral, safe environments, allowing people to do research without making a commitment.

At these seminars, people also have an opportunity to observe the advisors and assess if they'd be interested in forming a relationship. Can the advisors explain financial concepts well? Are they polite? Would the personalities work well together? They can also meet others who already have a relationship with an advisor and provide firsthand experiences or referrals.

Attending seminars is an alternative approach to interviewing advisors in the captive environment of their offices and perhaps feeling pressured to make a commitment. Just thinking about going to an office and divulging their private financial information can make many people feel uncomfortable and stop them from getting advice.

Several investment companies allow people to open an account and invest online. (Visit www.marketwatch.com to learn what the top-ranked online investment companies are.) Of course, those new to investing may need someone to help assess the options and develop a financial plan.

> You'll find that investing isn't all that complicated as you begin to learn more about it.

"I Don't Have the Money to Invest"

When I see people talking on their expensive smart phones and hear them discuss the high monthly rates, I think, "There's an extra $100 a month that could be going into an IRA contribution." That would be one way to "find the money" to max out 401(k) plans or contribute the maximum amount to IRAs. As an example, Mr. Earl had a fondness for expensive silk ties but he gave up buying them in order to purchase his few shares of stock at a time.

> To "find money," scrutinize your spending behavior and find ways to redirect your money. I call this "behaving your way to wealth." In order to behave your way to wealth, simply change a habit, like buying magazines every week or coffee every day, and redirect the money to savings. The level of sacrifice you make depends on how badly you want your dream.
>
> What are you willing give up to find extra money for investments?

Analyze Your Spending

The first time I analyzed my spending, I was surprised by how much I really spent on eating out and buying clothes, plus I decided my dry cleaning bill was too high. I changed those habits. Building wealth is an inside job that requires mental preparation and making choices like I did. One of the callers to my radio show said it well: "I simply got sick and tired of living paycheck to paycheck."

The American Savings Education Council distributes a wonderful calculator to help people see how changing spending habits can add up over time. One side of the calculator lists a number of items that most people spend their money on, such as candy, snacks, lunch, and lottery tickets. These items may not seem to cost much, but the calculator forces users to see how much they actually spend each day. The other side of the calculator demonstrates how those mere nickel and dimes add up to thousands of dollars over time. (Visit www.choosetosave.org to request a calculator.)

The first step to finding "nickels and dimes" is to keep track of where your money goes. The process doesn't have to be overwhelming. A simple 3x5 notebook in your pocket is all you need. Write down every dime you spend and, at the end of the day, add up the total and look for patterns. Where is your money going? Are you spending your money eating out, or buying newspapers, magazines, and snacks? Once you identify your expenditures, you can begin to pinpoint the expendable "silk tie" in your budget.

If you don't have a budget, put making one on your priority "To Do" list and get started. Budgets provide another way to stay in control of your life. Any budget has fixed expenses, such as your mortgage, car note, insurance, and utilities. While you can sometimes spring money loose by renegotiating interest on loans, for example, it's discretionary expenses—groceries, clothing, entertainment, and gasoline—that wreak havoc on a budget. These discretionary expenses present opportunities to find money to invest. When it comes to finding nickel and dimes, a budget becomes your treasure map. With a few simple shifts in spending, you can find an extra $200 to invest each month.

I urge you to keep your adjustments realistic; don't set yourself up for failure using a bare bones approach unless you are motivated and disciplined enough to do it. Rather than eliminate an activity altogether, find a low-cost alternative. This will save you a lot of money.

Sample: *Show Me the Money*

Expense	Cost / Month	Alternative	Cost / Month	Savings
Cable TV	150.00	Basic Cable+ Netflix or Hulu	75.00	75.00
Cell phone	100.00	Limited Data/calling/ Friends and family	50.00	50.00
Health club	60.00	Exercise equipment (one-time investment)	60.00	60.00
Lunch	120.00	Brown bag 3 days a week	48.00	72.00
Totals	430.00		233.00	237.00

Move Forward with a Plan

It's all about tradeoffs. Just as there's a tradeoff between risk and reward, the same holds true when spending less today to invest in dreams for tomorrow.

Here's what an extra $200 a month can accomplish:

$200	10 Years	15 Years	20 Years	30 Years
4%	$28,000	$49,000	$73,000	$139,000
8%	$36,000	$70,000	$118,000	$300,000
10%	$41,000	$84,000	$153,000	$455,000
12%	$46,000	$100,000	$199,000	$705,000

Some people don't have enough money every month to cover the basics or are hindered from finding money to invest. This challenge is real and it's also doable. Like Mr. Earl, it may be that they simply don't make enough to invest. The answer? Mr. Earl realized early on that after covering his expenses, he needed to "up his income" to start investing.

Once you've tracked your spending and established your budget, if you've determined there's no extra money to be found, you may need to boost your job skills and salary, start a side-business, or get a part-time job. There are many ways to earn extra money. Remember, you don't need that much to invest each month.

Creating Extra Income

Here are ways people have created extra income for themselves:

1. Increase Job Skills

Lifelong learning is an essential life skill. Changes in the marketplace happen with lightning speed, and a person's skill-set can rapidly become obsolete. Companies often train their employees for higher-paying positions.

Does your company offer training? Talk with your supervisor to find out what you can do to be promoted. When you do it, remember to use at least part of your added income for investing—*after* contributing the maximum amount allowable to your 401(k).

Attaining higher education no longer requires attending school during the day or even on campus. Many universities now offer distance education and online learning, some of which is free if you are not seeking a degree or certification. Although tuition has risen, it's easier than ever to fund education with scholarships, loans, and grants.

To find out more about online learning and educational financing, visit *www.petersons.com* and *www.finaid.org.*

2. Start a Side Business

Many people increase their living by selling products like cosmetics, kitchenware, and household goods in their spare time.

3. Get a Part-time Job

Mr. Earl looked down the street and knew that each of those businesses could use his services. He also had a love for landscaping and took great pride in cleaning buildings. Happily, he found his nickel and dime jobs on the same street as the bank.

Follow Mr. Earl's example and earn your investment money doing something in your natural skill-set or passion. Many companies need part-time staff. Think about the businesses you frequent each week when you shop, bank, or work out. They already know you. Ask if they need part-time help. Who knows, maybe the gym where you work out will hire you and throw in a free membership. Then you can direct the money that you usually pay for membership toward your investment plan. The opportunity you need is right in front of you.

Many solutions won't require changing your lifestyle because you are already accustomed to living on your current income. For example, if your next pay raise is 5 percent and you're earning $50,000, that's an extra $2,500 a year that you can use to invest in a Roth IRA. According to the IRA chart, this allows you to save an additional $80,000 in 10 or 15 years—even more if you commit to investing your pay raises every year.

Mr. Earl earned less than $25,000 a year at the time of his semi-retirement. He proves that you really do have what you need. If Mr. Earl can achieve financial security, you can too!

-chapter 4-

Learn To Earn

Wealthy Appetite: The Habit of Lifelong Learning

"I didn't know enough to be afraid," Mr. Earl explained. He simply observed wealthy customers' behavior and followed suit. He listened to stockbrokers discuss the market and watched how the wealthy customers responded. They never panicked; instead, they added more stock certificates to their safe-deposit boxes. He listened to them discuss how many shares of a particular stock they owned and what type of dividend they could expect. Basically, Mr. Earl observed that wealthy people invested their money regardless of the ups and downs of the economy or the stock market.

The financial and corporate scandals of the early 2000s, followed by the devastation of the Great Recession, have shaken the confidence of average investors. They read their mutual fund and employee retirement plan statements and assume that their money has been standing still as if on a treadmill, or even losing value as if falling off a cliff. It may appear that your money is standing still or losing value but, in fact, it is actually working on your behalf.

Throughout the years, I often asked Mr. Earl what he thought about the current state of the economy or stock market. In response, he changed the subject, opting to share his latest investment opportunity with me. By doing that, he showed he wasn't interested in the day-to-day gyrations of the market. Instead, he operated from the valuable observation he'd made in the bank's parking lot——that building wealth has *little* to do with ups and downs of the economy or the stock market. Building wealth has *everything* to do with investing. That's how wealthy people put their money to work. Working class people save their money in the bank; wealthy people invest their money in stocks and bonds.

Osceola's Savings

When I first heard the story of Osceola McCarty, after whom the Department of Labor's Super Saver Award was named, I wondered how her savings might have grown if she had invested in stocks. Here was a woman who worked from sun-up to sundown washing and ironing clothes. She rarely left her home except to go shopping or make deposits at the bank. Earning only a few cents for cleaning each bundle of clothes certainly didn't leave much for saving.

While saving $280,000 represents no small feat, the comparison between Mr. Earl and Ms. McCarty indicates how money works. Mr. Earl represents a real-life example of what happens when people invest their money in stocks. By studying each of their stories, you can begin to understand the relationship between risk and return.

Risk is Relative

Gradually, Mr. Earl transferred his money from the bank to the stock market while Ms. McCarty continued to invest her money in savings accounts and certificates of deposits (CDs). Her money earned interest or "income." Over the years, those earnings compounded through the reinvestment of the interest income, and accumulated to several thousand dollars.

Mr. Earl, on the other hand, put his money into stocks. He invested his money for "growth," as he anticipated the stock price to increase over the years. In addition, the stock he chose to invest in paid dividends—another form of income. It's through dividends that his two shares of IBM stock grew to more than 250 shares over a 20-year period.

Savings vs. Investing

Let's compare how these two types of assets perform over time. In the case of Mr. Earl, two shares of IBM that cost him $318 grew to be worth more than $30,000 over 20 years. If he had deposited his money in a savings account with its historical average of 4 percent interest, his $318 investment would be worth a mere $1,050 today.

In Ms. McCarty's case, she earned an average of 4 percent on her money in CDs. She was able to save more than $280,000 over her lifetime, and yet the return she realized was slightly above inflation. Although her principal or investment was not at risk, she had assumed "inflation risk."

You have choices when deciding to invest your money. You have to determine your goal: growth, income, or a combination of the two?

Whether you put your money to work for income or growth will depend on how much time you have and how much risk you are willing to take. Both Ms. McCarty and Mr. Earl invested their first nickels and dimes in the bank because it was safe. In effect, they lent their money to the bank, which paid them a fee in the form of interest.

Depending on the type of investment you make, you assume one type of risk or another. Of course, there are tradeoffs in every investment you make. Understanding those tradeoffs can help you

The Inflation Factor

Ten years ago, a loaf of bread cost about $2 at the grocery store. Today, a low-priced loaf of bread costs $4.00. That means in 10 years, a loaf of bread has almost doubled in price.

Has your income increased 50 percent in the past 10 years? Even if it has, your salary is simply standing still because the cost of covering all of your basic needs continue to increase. These needs include housing, automobiles, gasoline, natural gas, food—the list goes on and on. Because inflation has averaged 3 percent annually, your money has to earn interest at the rate of inflation to simply stay ahead of the game.

This stresses the importance of knowing how inflation affects your overall return. If your money can't buy as much as it once did, then you're risking your ability to maintain your standard of living. Again, risk is relative.

Putting Your Money to Work

By investing in IBM stock, Mr. Earl wanted to put his money to work for growth, which means he wanted the value of the stock to rise or "grow" in value. Over the past 30 years, stocks have earned an annual rate of return of just over 10 percent. By putting his money to work in stocks, he had the potential to earn a 10 percent historical rate of return. This is a major reason his portfolio grew to nearly a million dollars by early 2014. Clearly, his earnings grew far above the rate of inflation.

"Stock" Pile Your Money?

Although Mr. Earl's portfolio experienced several downturns in 30 years, his investment in IBM stock serves as a great example of how investing in big companies for the long term can build wealth in spite of the risk involved.

Why did Mr. Earl chose IBM stock? Because he learned it was a "blue chip" stock, which is simply a stock issued by a corporation that is both large and has been consistently profitable for several years. If you play poker, you know that the blue chip is the most valuable chip, which is where the term comes from.

A company issues stock initially to help finance its growth into the future. Its current revenues or profits might not be enough to finance its future growth. Rather than take out a loan from the bank or issue debt in the form of bonds, it issues stock and allows individuals to become part owners or "shareholders." By purchasing shares of the stock, people are able to share in the benefits of the company's growth.

A company's stock price usually reflects how well the company is performing. If the company does well and increases its profits, the price of the stock increases. If it's unprofitable, the stock's price falls to reflect the company's poor performance. While factors such as the economy and the overall stock market also have an influence, the share price generally indicates how well a company is performing.

The Secret to Accumulating Wealth

Over the years, IBM's stock value has been up and down. In the mid-1980s, it lost more than 60 percent of its value and employees were laid off as the company restructured to stay competitive. Many shareholders sold their stock because they were afraid it wouldn't recover its value. Does this sound familiar? Even blue chip stocks hit bumps in the road, which is why it's sound advice to only invest money that you can afford to put at risk.

During that downturn, Mr. Earl continued to have his dividends reinvested in more shares of IBM. Instead of panicking, he felt overjoyed because those dividends could buy more shares at the declining price. In fact, he learned that volatility can be the greatest secret to accumulating wealth. Reinvesting the dividends helps investors deal with that volatility and experience the magic of compound growth, which Albert Einstein considered the "eighth wonder of the world." Where did Mr. Earl adopt the outlook that downturns in the market are opportunities to purchase more shares? From the wealthy bank patrons he got to know. Stocks have historically outperformed any other type of investment over long periods of time, averaging between 10 and 12 percent annually for the past 70-plus years. Clearly, this result doesn't happen every year. The market might go up 20 percent one year and down 10 percent the next. That's why investing for the long term is essential.

Getting comfortable with this type of market risk is the most important lesson of all because your ability to continue to invest over the long term will determine your success. Which type of investment you choose depends on your goal for the money and when you need access to your money. After answering these questions, you should be able to determine how much risk you can take. Understanding the difference between saving and investing is essential in order to master the art of building wealth. If you're accumulating money for a specific purpose such as purchasing a car or making a down payment on a home and you'll need access to your money within five years, then you "save" your money. If your purpose is for retirement funding or financial security and your time frame is more than five years, then it's wiser to "invest" your money. But before you invest, put money aside in case of emergency.

How Money Works

**If you learn how to put
your money to work for you,
eventually you won't have to work at all.**

chapter 5
Create Your Future Each Day

Wealthy Focus: The Habit of Achieving Goals

Goals Are Dreams with Deadlines

I attribute Mr. Earl's financial success to connecting his emotional need for financial security to a specific goal. If building wealth were as simple as reading a book or attending a seminar, most Americans would be millionaires. But in order to achieve anything of significance, we need to have strong internal or emotional reasons for doing so. It's the fuel that propels us forward in the face of unforeseen obstacles or uncontrollable circumstances. In Mr. Earl's case, stock certificates represented much more than wealth to him. It represented independence.

What motivated Mr. Earl? I learned that, at the age of three, he had lived with his siblings in an orphanage for a few years when his mother suffered from tuberculosis. She eventually recovered and brought the family back together. "If it had not been for the charity of the Catholic Church, our lives would have been a lot worse," he recalled. He shared that memory with me when we visited a public school where he volunteers. This school was formerly the orphanage where he lived.

Achieving his dream of owning 1,000 shares of stock meant he could protect his children from having to experience a similar type of hardship. He wanted them to have options and choices. Clearly, his work ethic, faith, and outlook on life were shaped by his early childhood experiences.

My husband and I were the first to attend college in our families. We understood the value of a college education and wanted to make sure we could afford to send our children there, too. When our son Brandon was born, we invested in a pre-paid college tuition program. Michigan was one of the first states to offer a program allowing people to pay for tuition based on a projected cost in the future.

As a young married couple, we hadn't yet established any concrete financial goals, but we knew a college education meant a lot. Our need to provide our children with opportunities was the "internal" or emotional connection that motivated us to borrow $6,000 and buy in to a four-year college education program when our son was an infant. Paying the $200 monthly loan payment for three years put a dent in our budget, but by the time our son entered preschool, we had funded his four-year college education. We tackled saving for a four-year college education with $200 a month. It simply required three years of "acting small."

If you want to achieve your financial dreams, begin by making an emotional connection. What financial dreams can you emotionally connect to? Harness its fuel to make your dreams a reality. Of course, dreaming alone won't make it happen.

Acting Small

I learned that Mr. Earl took the principle of "acting small" to another level. He first invested in two shares of IBM stock, with the intention of eventually owning 100 shares of IBM. After buying those first two shares of stock, he calculated what the dividend paid and signed up for the dividend reinvestment program. Then he added more nickel and dimes until he owned a "round lot" or 100 shares. I remember first questioning his approach, thinking "Is he for real?" until years later when he'd call into the radio show to remind us of his progress. I can't think of a better expression to sum up the mathematical process of "acting small."

Mr. Earl could relate to acting small because his mother taught him how to save something from his pay every week. When a fellow employee told him he could have money deducted out of his paycheck, he invested it in his employer's stock. The opportunity to invest in stock directly from his paycheck made a lot of sense, so he started having a few dollars deducted every week. When he received the first statement, he was thrilled at how easy this was. This experience of investing in his employer's stock purchase program opened his eyes to the fact that he didn't have to pay the broker a commission like he did when he purchased IBM stock.

At the same time, he discovered he could put something away every week in his employer's retirement plan. The same types of mutual funds that he had invested in with the broker were available through payroll deduction, again without brokerage fees. So he started investing very small amounts because he wanted to make he sure he could pay Catholic school tuition for his children and cover his bills. However, today, these initial small seeds put into his employer's 401(k) plan and stock purchase program account for more than 40 percent of his portfolio, far surpassing his goal of owning 1,000 shares of stock.

Although Mr. Earl had access to brokers who had offices in the same building as the bank where he worked, it took him more than 10 years before he summoned the courage to ask them for help. Mr. Earl was a product of his generation. No one in his family had ever invested in stock before, which is also true for many who called into my radio program and said that investing is only for rich people. Mr. Earl experienced that same anxiety. Initially, he didn't believe the brokers would take him seriously as an investor. The few hundred dollars he had to invest was a lot of money to him, but only peanuts to them.

> The most important factor in building wealth is time. Don't fall into the trap that many investors succumb to—waiting until they have enough money to invest. Begin with whatever amount you can. If it's saving your chump change at the bottom of your purse or nickels and dimes you throw on top of your dresser drawer, then so be it. The major key to your success is taking action, even if it's small.

The Benefit of Retirement Accounts

Remember when reviewing Mr. Earl's portfolio, I was perplexed that Mr. Earl's IRA accounts were worth more than his 401(k) accounts after 20 years? That's when I knew he was an unusual man. Rarely would IRA accounts be worth more than retirement accounts if a person worked for the same employer for more than 30 years, as he did. But remember, his earnings were less than $20,000 a year during most of his employment (and 401(k) contributions are based on a percentage of earnings), whereas he could initially contribute $2,000 (now $4,000, more if you're over 50) annually to an IRA.

The question is: How did he find the money to contribute the maximum amount to his IRA? He earmarked income from specific nickel and dime jobs toward his IRA contributions. Some of his cleaning jobs paid less than $20 dollars a week. However, when he added the income together, he earned $200 or so a month. Those hundreds of dollars allowed him to contribute the maximum to his IRA accounts. He then invested those contributions into mutual funds and stocks, which grew to be worth more than his employer's 401(k) plan.

Many people make the mistake of contributing only the amount their employer will match in their retirement plans at work. For example, some employers offer to match, dollar-for-dollar, a percentage of the amount the employee contributes. Often people believe incorrectly that it doesn't make sense to contribute additional amounts. However, when you look at the principle of acting small, you see how small amounts can affect your savings over time. Couple that with the fact that your contributions to your employer-sponsored plan are tax deductible. Not only are you leaving potentially tens of thousands of dollars on the table, you're also paying more taxes. That means an additional $50 added to your employer plan each paycheck could mean an extra $50,000 over 20 years!

Investing in very small amounts was an extremely difficult concept for me to comprehend in my first conversations with Mr. Earl. But after reviewing his portfolio, I saw the principle of "dreaming big and acting small" in living color. Also, Mr. Earl would not have achieved the same amount of success if he'd not invested in stocks. Small amounts really do add up. A college education, down payment on a home, or financial security is simply nickels and dimes over time. If Mr. Earl can do it, you can too!

It's easy to act small. You can begin an investment program with as little as $10. However, $10 might not seem like it can make much of an impact. Can investing $10 or $20 at a time make a difference? Look no further than Mr. Earl. After all these years, Mr. Earl still buys one or two shares of stock at a time and calculates how many additional shares he will accumulate through the dividend reinvestment program. Dreaming big and acting small over a continuous period of time has been the secret to his success.

Dream Big! Act Small!

One nickel,

One dime;

One share of stock at a time!

-chapter 6-

Don't Follow The Crowd

Wealthy Mindset: The Habit of Viewing Problems as Opportunities

Let's take a look at the events that have transpired since the 21st century began. While we were focused on Y2K and holding our computers responsible for ending the world, the stock market entered a period that compares to the stock market crash of 1929. The Internet/dot.com bubble burst and highflying technology stock prices plummeted, bringing the value of blue chip stocks down with them. Then the Great Recession hit, and some people are still dealing with the fall-out from that event.

In the early 2000s alone, Enron fell from grace and became synonymous with corporate scandal. Plus let's not forget the now-defunct Arthur Andersen accounting firm and subsequent downfall of MCI World Com, Adelphia, and Global Crossings. A host of other companies had to restate their earnings and the financial analysts who touted technology stocks were suspected of having ulterior profit motives of their own. This was followed by the housing crisis, bank bail-outs, high un- and under-employment and, of course, a falling stock market.

This sad state of affairs made seasoned investors run for cover. Given that some years have passed and stocks have recovered, we realize that investors who sold their stocks did so at the absolute worst time. Money pouring out of mutual funds hit record bottom levels by the spring of 2009, the lowest point of the market's Great Recession decline.

Making Lemonade

At the height of the technology bust, I asked Mr. Earl how he felt about his Lucent Technology stock losing 90 percent of its value. He replied, "I received Lucent shares as a result of the Baby Bells splitting up. They had a good run and I still think it's a good stock and will turn around in the future." That's what I call making lemonade out of lemons! I attribute his ability to stay the course with the fact that his conservative, diversified portfolio was not affected too negatively because Lucent made up only a small part of it. His blue chip stocks, including IBM and Exxon, declined, but not nearly as much as his technology stocks did. Indeed, Mr. Earl didn't follow the crowd in or out of technology stocks. Rather, he developed a different point of view from watching and listening to the bank's wealthy customers every day.

Stock Speculation

Thirty years ago, having just earned my securities license, my greatest fear was losing my clients' investment money on poorly selected stocks. In the early 1980s, personal computers gave way to all kinds of speculation. That's when I first invested in semi-conductor stocks like Seagate Technology and LSI Logic. In this arena, stocks commonly doubled in value in a month. Similar to the Internet bubble, everyone thought the economy was experiencing "a major shift from an industrial to a technological age." The personal computer would change everything.

During that time, I would dream about the stock market crashing. Well, in 1983, I watched as those investments lost more than half of their value—and the rest is history. I actually received the outcome I'd expected. In fact, I felt relief as I sold those stocks and carried capital losses forward for years to come. Little did I know that 20 years later, LSI Logic and Seagate Technology would become leaders in their industries and purchased for a pretty penny by large companies. The personal computer did indeed change everything; it just didn't happen overnight. Needless to say, those few thousand dollars I'd invested in technology stock in the 1980s would have been worth hundreds of thousands today. But I expected to lose money and therefore created my outcome.

In 1981, around the time I was investing in semi-conductor stocks, Mr. Earl found the nerve and the money to make his first investment. He had observed parking lot activity for more than a decade before he found the courage to approach a broker and make his first investment. He knew that he needed a lot of money to have a broker establish an account for him. Brokers often brag saying, "My clients need at least $100,000 before I'll give them advice." The fact that he didn't have much money didn't discourage Mr. Earl, however. He continued to ask questions and observe the wealthy customers at the bank. For example, when they needed a loan, they opened their safe-deposit boxes and used their stock as collateral. Mr. Earl had visualized visiting his private safe-deposit box where he would put 1,000 shares of stock that he would one day own. That represented wealth in his mind and he fully expected to own them. It's what wealthy people did, after all. I realized that, just as my outlook had created my outcome, so did his.

A Losing Lesson

My early experience as a broker influenced my future approach to investing. You see, if I had been as observant as Mr. Earl, I would have noticed that the veteran stockbrokers in my office steered clear of high-risk stocks. Most invested their clients' and personal fortunes in solid blue chip stocks. While I was investing in semi-conductor stocks, they invested in IBM and Procter & Gamble. Losing money investing in the stock market at the beginning of my career taught me an excellent lesson and established the conservative approach I take toward investing today. My outlook changed, too. Today, I fully expect my investments to create wealth over the long term.

Mr. Earl knew that he wouldn't become wealthy overnight. But he recognized that if he hung in there, he could be successful, too. Seeing the price of his IBM shares fluctuate in value and then watching those dividends buy more shares every quarter opened his eyes. My experience with investors has shown me most people can't duplicate Mr. Earl's success because they get in their own way, reacting emotionally to the rise and fall of the markets. I contend that the ability to build wealth doesn't require technical know-how. As Mr. Earl demonstrated, it requires an emotional intelligence that you can't learn in a book.

> Think about how you react when the market goes down. Do you get scared and want to sell your stocks? When you see the growth in your investments, do you become so elated that you spend your profits? Respond in either manner and you will not experience success like Mr. Earl did. Those two shares of IBM purchased in 1981 grew to more than 250 shares by 2004 because Mr. Earl controlled his emotions. He could have sold his shares out of fear or greed many times over.

I remember a time when the demise of IBM seemed imminent. In 1989, I had completed management training at an investment firm and was transferred to San Francisco shortly after the city had suffered a devastating earthquake. The recession of the early 1990s had just taken hold and jobs were scarce. IBM stock had been trading at over $100 a share, but by 1993, it was valued at only $13 a share.

My office was one block from IBM's headquarters on Market Street. I remember that several of the laid-off employees visited our investor center to roll over their retirement plans and many had several thousand shares of IBM stock. Their entire life savings had plummeted so much that these laid-off people had to sell their stock at rock-bottom prices to live until they found another job.

I asked Mr. Earl why he hadn't sold his stock when it lost so much of its value at this time. He said, "Ms. Debbie, I was trying to figure out how I could scrape up a few dollars to buy more shares of IBM.

When I looked at my statement, all I saw was how many more shares I was able to buy with my dividends."

Mr. Earl was able to control any fear of loss by seeking opportunity rather than catastrophe. By keeping a positive outlook and focusing on accumulating small amounts over time, he was able to attain his goal of owning 1,000 shares of stock.

If you change the way you look at things, the things you look at change.

It worked for Mr. Earl and it will work for you, too!

-chapter 7-

Just Set It And Forget It

Wealthy System—The Habit of Automation

"He was pulling out statements from everywhere. I don't believe he knew how much his portfolio was worth." This is how I describe to my seminar audiences what happened at Mr. Earl's dining room table when I conducted his portfolio review.

Mr. Earl knew that financial security would take time and effort, but he set up his success when he set up a failsafe plan: automatic investment programs. "Put something away from your pay every week," his mother had advised. The statements he'd haphazardly placed in the drawers of his dining room buffet were from dividend reinvestment programs that he'd not paid much attention to. This demonstrated another key to his success: The ability to "set it and forget it."

I laugh when people tell me they review their investments weekly. The so-called "active investors" display their portfolio holdings on their computer screens where they can review performance every day, hour, or minute. When Mr. Earl began investing in 1981, there was no CNBC, CNNfn, or 24-hour cable networks. The Dow Jones Industrial Average was never quoted on the evening newscast and few personal finance radio talk shows existed. But I believe watching your stock minute by minute can be hazardous to your wealth.

The media has made access to information about investing widely available to every household in America. It's great! People can have more information than ever before. On the other hand, this can be considered terrible if it causes people to make careless decisions. Every company will hit a bump in the road. For example, a company could introduce a new product that doesn't sell, or the company might not meet its financial targets in a certain quarter. These events could cause a stock price to decline in the short term. Responding to these short-term developments has caused "in the know" investors to sell their stock when it didn't turn out to be a good long-term decision. After all, Apple Computer, IBM, and McDonald's have all experienced their stock prices decline, only to recover by correcting their marketing strategies.

Don't Get Pulled Off Course

It's important to avoid any "noise" that might pull you off course. Noise is everywhere and can easily distract you from achieving financial success. To build wealth successfully, behave like Mr. Earl and learn to "set it and forget it" rather than respond to opinions all around you.

Noise gets disguised in many different forms: market volatility, negative economic news, outside influences, and more. It can become a nightmare if investors respond to unforeseen circumstances by panicking or trying to time the market.

When to Invest

When it comes to investing, the only guarantee is that interest rates, the market, and the economy will go up and down. They always have and they always will. Indeed, not knowing exactly how the market will behave makes investing interesting. People often ask me, "When is the best time to invest?" My response is, "When you have the money." I say that because no one can predict the future. What's needed is a positive outlook and a basic understanding of how financial markets work.

Yet it's not enough to have a positive outlook. Though it's difficult, it's important to stay the course, especially if investments decline by more than 50 percent in one year. However, that actually occurs on paper; investors don't make or lose money until a transaction occurs. My conversation with Mr. Earl regarding IBM's precipitous fall in the early 1990s comes to mind. That's when he said, "Ms. Debbie, I wish I could have bought more shares." After consulting with his broker and other investors to determine if he should sell his shares, he had no intention of selling the stock. His experience taught him that the dividends from IBM would allow him to purchase more shares because the price was much lower. Mr. Earl knew the benefits of setting it and forgetting it.

When to Sell

How do you know when to sell a stock? The answer comes from your research to determine if the fundamentals of the company have changed. In Mr. Earl's case, IBM had been a leader in computing. It had a phenomenal track record, had become too big and complacent, and needed new leadership. There was no scandal or fraud attached to its falling on hard times, therefore analysts believed it could recover. However, this wasn't the same situation with MCI WorldCom and Enron; they were trying to create revenues that didn't exist. The point is, get advice and conduct research before heading for the exit.

Choosing Investments

Other examples of noise include how high-flying stocks and mutual funds are touted in the media or advertised in personal finance magazines and newspapers. Keep in mind that those high numbers displayed indicate past performance, not future performance. More often than not, the stocks that are the leaders one year turn out to be the laggards the next.

Bet on the Jockey

For a company or a mutual fund to perform well, good management is necessary. This approach is called "betting on the jockey and not the horse." Lou Gerstner, the CEO hired to take on the daunting task of turning around IBM's fall from grace, had lots of practice "riding that horse." He had helped turn around RJR Nabisco and had headed American Express. Bill Miller, portfolio manager for the Legg Mason Value Trust fund and Bill Nygreen of the Oakmark fund family have consistently outperformed their peers because of their ability to identify and invest in strong-performing companies.

> Look for the winning jockeys in today's market and your horse might have a better run. Whether they manage a company or a portfolio, your job is to find good managers with whom to invest your nickels and dimes. Their track record and proven performance can give you the confidence to set it and forget it.

Index Funds

Another option is buying into an "index fund." An index fund simply invests in all the companies of a market index, like the S&P 500 or Russell 3000 index. Because they don't need to hire a portfolio manager or financial analysts to conduct research, management fees are much lower than funds that are actively managed.

Statistics show that fewer than 80 percent of mutual funds outperform their benchmark indexes. Many financial advisors believe that diversifying investments into different types of index funds can be an excellent low-cost approach rather than investing in actively managed mutual funds. There is certainly nothing wrong with having a portion of your investments in index funds, which perform just as well as actively managed funds. In fact, they are often offered as options in employer-sponsored retirement plans.

The objective of the index fund is to mirror the performance of the index—no more, no less. Many financial advisors and investors believe that their steady returns combined with reduced expenses are a fair tradeoff for the potential higher returns realized in actively managed funds. I do recommend them in the right situations.

The Static from Advertising

A lot of other sophisticated noise—like that coming from television and shopping mall advertising—can hinder good investment decisions. "Buy me, buy me" is the refrain heard subliminally—the kind of noise that keeps us awake in the wee hours of the morning with "infomercial" promises of a svelte figure or a miraculous cooking apparatus. Many people dial the advertised 800-number and, before they can change their minds, the item arrives on their doorsteps. That's how well this advertising noise can work.

Companies use sophisticated marketing to encourage people to take action. They know the profiles of their prospective customers and the propensity they have to buy certain items. But beware. Advertising noise can cause us to sabotage our ability to invest wisely. An emergency such as a car breaking down or roof leaking can deplete our investments and make it impossible to set it and forget it.

> Putting aside money for emergencies means you won't have to deplete your cash reserve earmarked for investments. Be sure you do it!

"Set-Off" Points

Some people can go into a discount store or mall with a list and purchase exactly what they've written on their lists. For them, the "set-off" points like advertising music piped into the store don't influence what they buy that day. But others get set off easily and respond to stimuli around them. They tell themselves they deserve a new trinket or toy—and spare no expense. They become the marketers' ideal buyers because they easily get caught in their advertising traps.

> The best antidote to overspending is to avoid the noise. Affirm your commitment to save the money for investments before you purchase any items, especially big-ticket ones, at the mall. Better yet, speed past the mall entrance altogether.

Frequent Market Updates

For some people, following market updates and looking up share prices makes them nervous. Therefore, it makes sense to review quarterly statements instead of checking the price of funds or stocks daily in the media. Remember that the longer the period of performance is compared, the more accurate assessments can be made.

> Looking at your investments daily or weekly and trying to determine performance is not based in reality. Take a much longer view. While "set it and forget it" does not mean you should ignore your portfolio, it does mean you need to give it time to grow automatically.

Emotional Investing in Cyberspace

It's great that the average person can invest using the Internet, but this unlimited accessibility can turn into another potential pitfall. When Mr. Earl has any concerns about his investments, he seeks advice from his broker and consults with other investors he knows and trusts. The true value of financial advisors is they can prevent investors from responding emotionally to outside influences. That's why it makes sense to establish a relationship with an investment professional to get help discerning fact from fiction and preventing poor decision-making.

You can still have the convenience of making transactions online while benefiting from having full-service investment relationships. Doing so allows you to reduce transaction costs when you don't use someone else's advice.

Using the Noise as an Advantage

Peter Lynch, the famous mutual fund portfolio manager, attributes one of his all-time greatest investments to an observation that his wife made while shopping at the grocery store (a form of noise). She noticed women were buying the "eggs" packaging that had panty hose in them. His research told him these stockings were made by Hanes, whose sales had increased significantly. With more women working in the 1970s and 1980s, they found that buying their personal wares in a grocery store was more convenient than having to go to a department store. Have you noticed any products or services that your family or friends have been raving about? Conduct your own research and determine if they might be a potential investment opportunity. Noise is everywhere and if you tune in carefully, you can be richly rewarded.

In the early 2000s, terrorist attacks and subsequent wars caused the market to be more volatile and made many investors quite nervous. Then the chaos and losses of the Great Recession were impossible to ignore. This noise has even made veteran investors uneasy. Yet Mr. Earl often finds opportunity in chaos and you can, too. For example, he called into the radio show and encouraged listeners to consider buying defense and security industry stocks. In fact, a year prior to the attacks that occurred on September 11, 2001, he suggested Martin Marietta as a stock to invest in through a dividend reinvestment program. Putting his money to work by investing it systematically and leaving it alone has been the secret to his success.

> The noise in the marketplace will always exist, both in negative and positive ways. It comes down to how you choose to respond to that noise when making your investment decisions.

Just Set It and Forget It!

It's not how much—it's for how long!

-chapter 8-
Leaving A Path For Others

Wealthy Legacy-The Habit of Paying It Forward

"You have a limited education and you won't go far working at this bank," a bank executive once told Mr. Earl as he took him aside and encouraged him to invest his money. He too, had been labeled a "slow learner" as a child and had overcome his learning disability. He "paid forward" the support he received by providing Mr. Earl with the encouragement he needed to pursue investing in stocks. If not for him, it may have taken another 10 years before Mr. Earl found the courage to purchase his first share of stock. Think of the amount of reinvested dividends and compounded interest he would have lost out on! That's why I believe it's so important to expose others to the world of investing.

After spending several years in the investment industry, I realized that so many people sat on the outside and looked in. When I began my career, I concentrated my energies on prospecting high net-worth clients who had assets of at least $100,000. I recall presenting a seminar to our existing high net-worth customers and their friends at an exclusive hotel in San Francisco. When I scanned the audience, I realized that the attendees didn't need more information on how to invest. They were already wealthy and clearly had mastered the principles of investing. They were taking advantage of the elaborate hors d'oeuvres and using these events to network with their peers.

I decided that the people who needed the most help were not privy to this exclusive event. That's why I created a radio show targeting average Americans, focusing my energies on investment education. However, Mr. Earl showed me that people need more than information. They need someone to take them by the hand and show them how to get started. They need to be brought "inside" and shown exactly what to do.

Get Others Started in Investing

Mr. Earl took "pay it forward" to a new level the day he offered to transfer one share at a time of a stock that he owns into the names of radio listeners so they could experience what it means to own stock. Frankly, I was really concerned about his approach. It seemed simple to transfer shares of a stock and have people reimburse the costs, but the paperwork could be complicated. He told me he was doing this to calm new investors' fears and get them started, saying, "Ms. Debbie, people need more than lip service—they need help." Once they received the share, they could enroll in the dividend reinvestment program and watch their shares accumulate. He suggested they also show people in their close circle how easy and sensible it is to invest. This showed Mr. Earl's generosity and abundant mindset.

The fact that he was an experienced and successful investor provided a tremendous amount of confidence to potential investors who listened to my program. More than that, it increased their comfort level. Of course, the share he transferred was of a large, well-known blue chip company; he told them to only risk money they could afford to lose—the same advice his mentor had given him before he purchased his first shares stock. Once again, Mr. Earl had made an astute observation, which I am simply passing on. Pay it forward.

Pay It Forward to Your Children

Remember in my initial review of Mr. Earl's portfolio, I listed several accounts that were in the names of his three children? He had invested in stocks and mutual funds for his children, opening IRAs for them. This is a great place to start.

I suggest the first place to pay it forward is to your children. They have the most important asset of all—time. In addition, they can experience "how money works" before they leave your household. I think this is the greatest gift that any parent can give their offspring. In addition, investing in a college savings plan for your children early—in fact, when they are born –can mean the difference between them attending the college of their choice or having to contend with debt from college loans. Visit *www.collegesavings.org* to learn what type of option your state provides.

Instead of piling the latest electronic games or designer clothing under the Christmas tree, give each of your children a share of stock from a company that makes their favorite gadget. (You can print off an actual certificate at *www.oneshare.com* or visit *www.directinvesting.com* and invest with the company directly.) Better yet, have your child do the research and determine if the latest fad indeed comes from a profitable enterprise. Being creative and paying it forward may produce a budding investment guru like the famous billionaire Warren Buffet.

Distribute Stocks as Gifts

Paying it forward can also be used to distribute gifts to your closest friends and colleagues. Graduations, weddings, birthdays, and childbirth can provide great opportunities. An "old school" gift was buying a savings bond for nieces and nephews on their birthdays. The "new school" approach is giving them the gift of a share of stock or making a deposit in their college savings fund..

Years ago, buying stock was a cumbersome process. Now, most companies allow buyers to establish accounts and purchase shares to gift to someone else online. The fee to register stock is minimal and enrolling in direct stock investment programs has never been easier. For example, Home Depot allows people to invest in their stock by visiting their website. How's that for do-it-yourself?

You can enroll in dividend reinvestment programs and direct stock investment programs by contacting the appropriate transfer agent. You can conduct research at your local library through the "Value Line Investment Survey" or "Standard and Poor Research." You can also find access to most of this information at *www.finance. yahoo.com.*

Paying a Home Forward

When my husband and I were first married, we had to start from an asset base of almost zero. But we were fortunate enough to purchase my mother-in-law's co-op town home when she decided to move into a senior citizen housing complex. It was in an excellent location and conveniently located next to the senior citizen apartment building she moved into. I believe she moved out because it was her one asset that she could pass on to her son.

Her co-op housing arrangement did not allow her to accumulate equity at the same rate as a conventional mortgage. As a result, my mother-in-law didn't receive much of a payout; much of the monthly co-op payment was applied to the maintenance of the units and surrounding areas. Yet the value of her gift is immeasurable as she paid forward a home. Simply transferring the ownership to us meant we didn't have to pay rent or to come up with a down payment in order to buy. With the recent housing crisis it is important to make sure you purchase a home you can afford. Many states provide homeownership counseling, down payment assistance, and mortgage financing options. Visit *www.hud.gov* to learn what programs are available.

Establish a Will

After conducting the portfolio review, I encouraged Mr. Earl to make a full account of his investments and establish a will. He didn't fully know how much he had invested and quickly realized it would be extremely difficult for his wife to know it, as well. The current values of his assets weren't enough to be assessed estate taxes, but if they continued to grow, his estate might be subject to taxes in the future.

When people die without a will, the results of years of sweat and effort rarely get distributed properly and may go unaccounted for.

It's best to put our financial houses in order so we can decide how to pay our assets forward at the time of our deaths. We should have a "last will and testament" filed away with our personal papers and copies held in a safe-deposit box outside of our home where they can't be destroyed prematurely. No one wants to talk about death, but let's face it: This is the only event that is guaranteed. Preparing a will simply provides another opportunity to pay it forward to the next generation.

Truly Self-Made?

I often hear people talk on and on about how they are self-made. But I believe it's not possible to be a "self-made" anything. If we've experienced success, it's the result of someone paying it forward. Even Mr. Earl had a co-worker who encouraged him to invest. He didn't make any assumptions about his ability to understand investing or whether he could afford it. Indeed, he knew he couldn't afford not to.

> It doesn't matter how much you earn today or whether you went to college or finished high school. Mr. Earl is living proof that you can build wealth on any income. You don't have to have an MBA in finance or earn six figures. The only possible obstacle is not believing that you have what it takes to nickel and dime your way to wealth. It's not hard, but it ain't easy.

Mr. Earl and Osceola McCarty were extraordinary examples of how anyone can nickel and dime their way to wealth. Their stories continue affect my life and the lives of countless others. I've learned more from their humble, gentle spirits and the importance of saving and investing than an MBA in finance could ever teach. Their lives validated the path that I chose in my quest to inspire others to build wealth. This story is my way of paying it forward.

Pass it on!

-chapter 9-
It's Never Too Late

"I had worked for the bank for almost 15 years before I got enough nerve to buy my first stock," Mr. Earl said, acknowledging that time got away from him. But he didn't allow his late start to determine his final destination.

If achieving financial security is our goal, then the decisions made today and going forward will determine our success. We need to face hard realities in the challenging economic environment that we live in. The days of working for one employer, retiring, and collecting a pension large enough to meet our needs for the rest of our lives are over. Mr. Earl proves that, regardless of our station in life, it's never too late to secure a financial future.

Because of medical and technological advances, people are living longer. Life expectancies will continue to increase. When the Social Security system was created 60 years ago, the life expectancy of a male was 63 years old. Quite frankly, the system was created with the intention of few people collecting full benefits for an extended period of time. But today, a man can expect to live 82 years on average and a woman almost 90. That's almost 20 years beyond the age of 67—the age which retirees can now collect full Social Security benefits. This means our money has to last a lot longer.

Add to that the fact that the average American has saved less than $10,000 for retirement. That means a lot of people will find themselves ill prepared financially. They'll be forced to make drastic changes in their lifestyles when they retire. To avoid this predicament, they're wise to follow Mr. Earl's example and take advantage of every opportunity to invest toward retirement—at any point in time!

> If you're a late-bloomer investor with retirement looming in the horizon, your choice becomes retiring later rather than sooner. You also have to make a conscious choice to commit more of your income to savings. What will you do?

Employer's Retirement Plan

While Mr. Earl's first investment was in an individual stock, when a co-worker told him he could invest in his employer's retirement plan, he was thrilled. Over the next 20 years, Mr. Earl was able to accumulate a sizable sum in his employer's plan.

I think it's best to invest in employers' retirement plans first, before any other investment. These plans allow us to gain an immediate tax deduction along with deferring taxes on the earnings. As an example, for every $100 put into this plan, the take-home pay is reduced by $60 on average. In addition, employers may match employee contributions dollar-for-dollar, 50 cents on the dollar, or another amount. That's free money! Consider employer-sponsored plans the first destination on the road to wealth.

> Don't make the mistake of contributing only the amount that your employer will match. Rather, stretch your finances so you can contribute the maximum amount allowable. If you don't, you're leaving money on the table because you're not taking full advantage of the tax benefits. Remember, the more you make, the more Uncle Sam takes. By contributing the maximum amount to your 401(k), you reduce your taxable income. It may not seem like much, but an additional $50 a month could add up to tens of thousands of dollars in the long run. Nickels and dimes really do add up.

Retirement Plans for the Self-employed

For those who don't have an employer-sponsored retirement plan, one can be created through an Individual Retirement Account (IRA), as explained in the next section. Self-employed people have even more options because of the number and types of retirement plans for the self-employed now available.

When Mr. Earl began his investment program more than 30 years ago, the self-employed retirement plan options were limited to a simplified employee pension plan (SEP-IRA) or a Keogh. Now people can establish their own personal 401(k) accounts and contribute over $40,000 a year, depending on their income.

In the past, these types of plans were cost-prohibitive because administrative costs ran to several thousand dollars annually. Now, a personal 401(k) can be set up for a few hundred dollars and provides access to hundreds of mutual funds or individual stocks. If Mr. Earl had the same opportunity, his SEP-IRAs would have been worth more than his employer-sponsored 401(k) plan. With the passing of the Tax Relief Act of 2001, the contribution percentages increased from 15 percent to 25 percent. Clearly, the incentives to save for retirement are greater than ever before.

Any income you earn that is not subject to withholding qualifies you to establish a self-employed retirement plan. If you play your cards right, you can have a 401(k), SEP-IRA, and a Roth IRA. Having many different baskets for your retirement savings is an excellent way to jumpstart your retirement savings.

Individual Retirement Accounts

After fully contributing to an employer-sponsored plan, it's wise to invest in an Individual Retirement Account (IRA). There are two types: traditional IRA or Roth IRA. Which one you choose depends on your particular situation. My rule of thumb is if you can deduct the contribution, then invest in the regular IRA. Otherwise, the Roth IRA offers an unbeatable benefit of making tax-free withdrawals at the time of retirement. (Tax advisors can help determine the best choices.)

One of the first observations I made during Mr. Earl's portfolio review was that his IRA accounts were valued at more than his employer-sponsored plan. This is unusual because ideally people contribute a lot more to their employers' plans than to IRAs. The reason that Mr. Earl's IRA accounts are worth more is because his wages at the bank were extremely low.

> If you've not taken full advantage of your employer retirement savings plans in the past, you, too, can leverage your other retirement savings options.

Saving for College vs. Retirement

Many parents are concerned about how to save for college and their retirement at the same time. Indeed, families have limited resources and must make difficult choices.

I believe the time to start saving for college is the day a child is born. That sounds good on paper but when families are paying a mortgage, car notes, day care, and school tuition, how many dollars are left for investing? Very few. Mr. Earl found a way to send all three of his children to Catholic school—and while paying off his mortgage. He did not, however, pay their college expenses because he couldn't afford them.

I suggest if a family has to choose between contributing to a retirement account versus a college savings fund, it's best to choose retirement savings. Here's why. A fully funded four-year college education is not a birthright. I believe there is nothing wrong with having young people work during the summer to save for their own college education and/or applying for financial aid. Hundreds of college loans and work-study programs are available to students from poor and middle-income families. The only debt that pays a proven return is financing college, and now, with the current crisis in crushing debt from student loans, it is also important to take steps to ensure that that debt is no greater than absolutely necessary.

Far too often, I've seen the results of parents who've jeopardized their future for their children's college education. The best gift you can give your children is the ability to take care of yourself during your retirement years without becoming a financial burden to them. Plus the values your children can learn from investing in themselves are priceless.

Just Get Started

Ideally, the best time to begin a retirement savings program is when you're young. However, age has its advantages when it comes to saving for retirement. The Tax Relief Act of 2001 included several caveats. For example, the "retirement catch-up" provision makes it possible for workers age 50 or older to contribute additional money into their retirement plans. Late bloomers can now contribute $500 more into an IRA account or an additional $1,000 in their employer sponsored plans.

Our political leaders today recognize the challenges our country's existing Social Security system will face in light of the coming explosion of eligible retirees who will qualify for benefits. Specifically, fewer workers will be paying into the system and more retirees will be drawing from it, creating a crisis that will have to be solved. The solution, in my view, is to start putting those nickel and dimes into personal retirement plans.

> Begin where you are. The more you can invest toward retirement, the greater your ultimate results will be. It doesn't matter what amount you begin with; it only matters that you start. Remember, it's not about how much; it's about for how long.
>
> Think of the sacrifice Mr. Earl made when his income was less than $1,000 a month. "My wife thought I was throwing money away by investing," he said. In the early stages, you may not see much progress and it can seem like you're on a treadmill going nowhere. But start with nickels and dimes, and make a commitment to invest at least 10 percent of your earnings. As they increase, earmark all your pay raises and extra income toward your investments. When you do this, you're well on your way to building a retirement income.

Play Retirement Catch Up

The most important factor in experiencing the type of success Mr. Earl has is the ability to act as soon as possible. Conversely, the worst thing is doing nothing. Okay, it may require having a nickel-and-dime enterprise and working for more years. But don't allow panic and regret to paralyze you. Instead, follow in Mr. Earl's footsteps.

It's possible to play retirement catch up, winning by leveraging our talents and taking advantage of opportunities. It also requires acting small—even just saving $25 a week or $100 a month and contributing to employer-sponsored plans and/or starting an IRA.

If you don't play the savings and investment game, you can't win.

Start with what's affordable now and increase the amounts from there. Remember, money can't buy time; it's never too late to start.

It's Never Too Late

Begin where you are!
If not now, when?

Resources

Below are some of the resources mentioned in this book, as well as a few others you might find of interest:

www.marketwatch.com

www.choosetosave.org

www.petersons.com

www.finaid.org

www.sharebuilder.com

www.collegesavings.org

www.directinvesting.com

www.hud.gov

www.finra.org

www.nasdaq.com

www.oneshare.com

Other books by Deborah Owens

A Purse of Your Own: An Easy Guide To Financial Security, Simon and Schuster Publisher

Kindle edition:
http://www.amazon.com/Purse-Your-Own-Financial-Security-ebook/dp/B0030MQJLY/ref=sr_1_3?s=books&ie=UTF8&qid=1399 295110&sr=1-3&keywords=deborah+owens

Confident Investing A Wealth Building Guide For Women
Owens Media Group LLC

Wealthy Radio podcasts are available at www.deborahowens.com

You can also contact Ms. Owens at www.deborahowens.com

About The Author

Deborah Owens is a thought leader and advocate for remedying the wealth disparities of women and minorities. She is the author of three books most recently critically acclaimed, *A Purse of Your Own: An Easy Guide to Financial Security*, published by Simon and Schuster. Owens is a 20-year Wall Street veteran and former vice president with Fidelity Investments. She a sought after speaker on the topics of: Wealth Building, Leadership, Entrepreneurship.

Ms. Owens is a media personality who has been a contributor to CNN, ABC News Now, News One Now, Shape, Essence Magazine, Ebony, Black Enterprise. She is host of Wealthy Lifestyle Radio, which airs on WEAA an NPR affiliate in Baltimore, MD.

Deborah Owens is CEO of Owens Media Group, which creates sales, leadership and financial education programs on multimedia platforms for organizations and companies. She holds a Master of Business Administration from Loyola University of Maryland.

Notes

Notes

Notes

Notes

41164449R00059

Made in the USA
Middletown, DE
06 March 2017